I0888950

FURTHEST ECOLOGY

The Mountain West Poetry Series

Stephanie G'Schwind & Donald Revell, series editors

FURTHEST ECOLOGY

Adam Fagin

POEMS

The Center for Literary Publishing
Colorado State University

For information about permission to reproduce
selections from this book, write to
The Center for Literary Publishing
attn: Permissions
9105 Campus Delivery, Colorado State University
Fort Collins, Colorado 80523-9105.

Printed in the United States of America.

Library of Congress Cataloging-in-Publication Data

Names: Fagin, Adam, 1979- author.
Title: Furthest ecology : poems / Adam Fagin.
Description: [Fort Collins, Colorado] : The Center for Literary Publishing,
Colorado State University, [2019] | Series: The Mountain west poetry series
Includes bibliographical references and index.
Identifiers: LCCN 2018057027 (print) | LCCN 2018057964 (ebook)
ISBN 9781885635686 (electronic) | ISBN 9781885635679 (pbk. : alk. paper)
Subjects: LCSH: Thayer, Abbott Handerson, 1849-1921--Poetry. | LCGFT: Poetry.
Classification: LCC PS3606.A26567 (ebook) | LCC PS3606.A26567 A6 2019 (print)
DDC 811/.6--dc23
LC record available at https://lccn.loc.gov/2018057027
The paper used in this book meets the minimum requirements of the
American National Standard for Information Sciences-Permanence of Paper
for Printed Library Materials, ANSI Z 39.48-1984.

1 2 3 4 5   23 22 21 20 19

Publication of this book was made possible by a grant
from the National Endowment for the Arts.

National
Endowment
for the Arts
arts.gov

If one could establish
an absolute power
of silence over oneself

—Lorine Niedecker

CONTENTS

SOLE INHABITANT

In 1896, Abbott Thayer, American painter and amateur naturalist, described the principle of countershading, "Thayer's Law," which said that an animal's coloring, dark on top and light underneath, distributed shadow equally across the body, making it appear flat and concealing it from predators. Thayer published a book on his discoveries, *Concealing-Coloration in the Animal Kingdom*. Its concepts would form the blueprint for military camouflage during WWI, earning Thayer his nickname, "the father of camouflage."

In 1910, the artist gave a lecture to a group of "doubting ornithologists" at the Smithsonian Institution. He showed that a hummingbird, when placed in a bush and seen from a pronghorn's perspective, as skylight merged with its white tail, produced an effect of visual "obliteration." When Thayer requested the group lie down to observe the hummingbird from the pronghorn's vantage point, they unanimously refused.

"I have been left alone in the world to point this out," wrote Thayer. His drafts and letters are homiletic journeys in which existential inquiry meets sketch of Satyr butterfly and bamboo moth. Transcribing glimpses of a nighthawk's wing, Thayer's language erupts on the page, revealing a mind in pursuit of what the artist considered a revolutionary vision of the natural world. "I bring evidence of concealing power," one page reads in its entirety, "no course open but to investigate."

(obliterate by coalescence)

LUSH MINIMALISMS

broken

light

broken

light

clearing

broken

light

crossing

openfield

blue-gray

light

entering

my

field

of vision

trading

                 sweetgrass

with

                 evening

light

                 I look

away

                 as indigo

foreshadows

                 violet

dark tipped whether

flowering gust

crossing parenthetical twilight

a minimal sky listens

with collapsed reverence

it listens in configurations

of silence interior to time

image line and frame

FIRST DREAM OF COLOR

I have learned

       all light comes

down through the

       motion of the observer.

It is only to the still

       observer that the mo-

tion of the observed
       form adds revealment.

To a motionless man,

any branch or leaf seams

       the same bright

shore.

*

A first sight be-

comes, when time

is visible, wholly

outside color. I enter

the animal, sucking

motion from the leaf-

like shadow of its wing.

Its true outline en

masse axis of fleshy

processes—"bird" being

a mistranslation of its

environment—pure leafy

space threads twilight

with thumb

and forefinger.

*

Dear northern region, dear dear one:

We hold these truths to be self-evident,

but they're merely exposed.

Meaning tumbles over green leaves.

Aix sponsa ascend a learned vacuity.

Detaching its velocity from hypertelic

rhythms of a redpoll,

a parched grammar tills the soil.

*

This is not a theory.

The sky is blue and there are tree-shadows on snow. It wings,

little white idylls, occupy a point further in. Here a straight line

extends the gaze. It's another blackbird heard across the range.

When reversed it's turned to evidence: I open the impression—

blue kite cut apart by moon-fragment—and am met by observation:

a flight where matter converges with its style of conveyance.

*

A leaf, a nest,

a web, a cry.

In this moment thought

multiplies the animal it becomes.

The sun makes total what it touches.

But only the artist can do this in total darkness.

FUGITIVE DEPTH

I inherit the thereness of the frame

a series of dislocations centerless

journeys and dead-ends through

which I look "for what is looking"

or watch my vision flicker between

internal horizon and ghost-

semantic shore

if I've seen something it

isn't something but *is* that

grows green in silvery sun I

want form to account for image

and perception's fluid entanglements

to force it to "Burst like a stream /

making a world how large do you

think it is / and how far?"

can I portray this process as

temporal vanishing point can

I sidestep its concentric geography—

erased from sight but not from

consequence as some are cast

into corporeal surface of a gaze

called *splay pastoral*

called *morphological ravine*

Watcher, it is inference

I search through:

robin's egg, green shade.

Perspective is divine

malfunction.

Form is an angle

of noon

       protruding

through a stalemate

of palette and

       circumference.

T'S LAW

If among the waxwing's flight, I describe unbroken light, I describe
water among the sleep of birds. A wingbeat governing swift fluidities
of form. Dear precious, dear dearest: Here I seize on a sea a pure
white vessel's breaking. Over many days mistaken for a cloud, a
man's eye creeps up the branches, eats the gray buds. He thinks
of white as his sun at night. Has he ever thought his impressions
are born? Pouring his confinement through a moon's milk stare,
first daylight drains this strange bird: attention residing in a nexus
of recurrence. Old ideas that cause the mind to live among bright
objects—but only as a means of concealment. Each glance is a
distance I simulate. When I require a political economy, I look
directly at the sun. Sucked through September's pulse, a solar hinge
no hand can touch, sound ascends daylight. The eye is made aware.
The boundary is birdsong filled with ghostly listening. Or the color
of the sea approaching the clairvoyance of the artist's attention.
Weaving his periscope from the dark of inquiry, it is made vessel by
faintly visible seashore. A painter is the world conscious that light
belongs there. Reductio ad absurdum. Until a parallel ear forgets. A
duplicate canvas engulfs silhouette with particle fire. Here a moment
of sculpture tears off its crisscross veil. Monadnock, my mountain
home: These rocks are thresholds that multiply Praxiteles. Where

dewdrops further elucidate the majority of tulips, root outweighs flower head, twilight, *Promethea Sphinx*. In the absolute detail it descends, a leaf's inverted vernacular. Out of which one ruptured katydid proceeds, eternally convex, transverse, beneath a breath of moonshine and meadow grass, a shadow's arrowy vehemence.

WHEN I LOOK

Monadnock

Those who simply climb to the peak of Monadnock have seen but little of the mountain. I came not to look off from it, but to look at it.

—Henry David Thoreau

Kate Thayer died in May 1891 after a long illness. "I take to [painting] all these dark months as to drink," wrote her husband Abbott at this time. A subject to which he returned devoutly was Monadnock, the New Hampshire mountain he lived beside for many decades. Described as Thayer's fetish and totem, he presented its crags and ledges in impressionistic blurs of snowy underbrush and finely detailed articulations of light intersecting its stately slopes.

But behind this pristine pastoral image lived the artist's melancholy and dread. Kate's sickness, complicated by a lung infection, produced in her husband a morbid fear of disease, which he sublimated into his studies of Monadnock. A repository for metaphors of health and vitality, they achieve a harmony of form and color. One can locate the peaceful solitude and clarity of mind the artist sought there. But, as if he'd attempted to purge them of an unknown contaminant, these angelic visions of the New England landscape often look like they'd been compulsively scrubbed, bleeding a barely suppressed desolation and vacancy.

"The whole question is how absolutely, how perfectly the artist sees this vision," wrote Thayer. In the word *absolutely*, he suggests a kind of aesthetic purity (or self-purification) through art-making, one that might allow him to defy time and turn away death through artistic greatness. In the context of Thayer's collected works—in and outside of painting—this word also reveals his absolutist tendencies, portending his increasingly fanatical quest with regard to concealing coloration: He had to convert the world to his vision.

But Thayer's crusade to prove his theories only amplifies the psychic cracks visible in the Monadnock paintings. Assembling his views of the mountain as a metaphorical bulwark against life's uncertainties, he constructed line by line a transcendent figure that might absolve him of his earthly trembling, colonizing its image with denial battling fear and grief. However placid the mountain appears in his work, however possessed of Arcadian majesty it might have seemed from his neighboring New Hampshire home, Thayer's paintings foreshadow a growing struggle between representation and reality reflected prismatically through his steadily declining sense of self.

a dawn
no Hylodes dreams
a yes or no

has of brightness

(the sun)

(the sun)
a sparrow

I now remember

an acre of

cheek-bones
imparting to

leaves, a husk
a passing thought

of the ravine—

robins everywhere—
don't answer

hands now

have a citizen

blue may be true
blue, viewed scarlet

the staple
become fluid—

and the sonorous
next morning

beyond this, I
extends continuous

bright across its searching

A MOUNTAIN IN SEVERAL BRUSHSTROKES

Empty space composes

        ghostwhitedawn.

Ghostwhitedawn

      paints blue-green valley,

           confusing as it arranges

      the figure-ground relationship.

Place is a process by

    which self becomes

      metaphor for the relating

    of self to

      no known address.

            Is this "I" as ecological

            defect?

I could describe

       the world as a mountain

of trouble in every direction.

       Then description

becomes mountainous,

       a phrase obscuring the tangle

of light at eye level.

       But if the present is

a landscape changed by

       my looking at it,

         I've got nowhere to

           go to watch its

       hurried metonym

    dissolve painterly

         affection.

What I lose myself to

        the mind chooses,

mystical infrastructure

        from the blame

            of ruin. A root as red

   rootless red as buries night

                in its never-flowering suggestion.

        Wide as apparition,

      dense as spruce.

The white; the spot in the midst of the dark tip retains, of course, its contour.

I simply mean that these patterns, here, that nowhere extend to the border. are the only ones that no background can obliterate by coalescence, as black does the black tip of the no 1 - and would do in the demoticus if I gave this time to repeat him on a black ground.

I send you this whole mass rather than wait in hope to pull it together.

I have made two more marvellous bird-skin landscapes, one that represents a Himalaya mountain gorge and which is all made of the splendid out skin of a Monal pheasant.

PHOTOGRAPH OF ABBOTT HANDERSON THAYER'S
PORTRAIT OF KATE THAYER, 1888–89

undressing

hyacinth

a little shadow

breaches—

roots turned up—

black earth virgin's bower

just look—

mind nature posture absence

perceiving

eyes true form—

likeness collapsing

representation

with its pathology

were she visible

only image is visible—

the downward glance

it seems such an indignity

her *changed face*

it is not the woman but

imagines her with death

white dress—

between expression and

the instant it portrays

as beauty becomes

what it sees shadows

right arm in white

water of sleeve—

no shore where she is

FEATHER FRAGMENTS FROM LETTER

"I came not to look off

from it, but to look at it,"

said Thoreau after

climbing Monadnock.

It isn't seeing but having

seen that opens perspective.

This opening doubles

back on what's perceived,

the threat under which I

appear dissolve deceive etc . . .

Does this mean that having

seen one shouldn't look?

What's the difference between

gaping openly and glaringly

obtuse? The difference between

descending that mountain and

staring down its circular path.

If I paint what I am,

not what I see—

image is blindness;

every glance

becomes a mountain.

If I limn its likeness,

do I look at it only insofar

as it completes an idea of

itself—an idea that once

out of view is painted out

of existence? Till painting

becomes an image addressed

to its absence. Till this absence

becomes my own.

CIRCADIAN INFERENCE

clouded

   clotted

      cloaked

  spirality—I

     take my place

       in blue est

         dusk   to

        si   ng

            to—

       is depiction

     breach or fever

       map or destination?—

   in pitchblack

simulacra's

parts unknown

my voyage

becomes

not pattern

or detour

not context

or essay

not pore

or border

or pastime

or retreat

but an inward

migration

full of its

effects

LONGWINGEDSEA

In November 1915, Abbott Thayer traveled from Monadnock to Liverpool, England. With the help of artist-friend John Singer Sargent, he secured a meeting with British officials. Thayer hoped to convince the War Office to adopt changes to the field uniform based on his theories, but recent letters from Sargent suggested this was impossible. The artist spent his trip showing his ideas to professors and other naturalists and avoided the War Office. Internalizing the devastation he found, Thayer went into a frenzy. While Sargent made Thayer's case to officials, Thayer visited his friends the Whelpleys in Oxford, traveling together to London. Alarmed by the artist's condition, the Whelpleys devoted themselves to his care. This didn't prevent Thayer's abrupt departure for Glasgow, however, and a meeting with two prominent zoologists—a frantic trip that produced a letter to the Whelpleys in which he makes the strange declaration of "Total heavenly triumph," a line prompting a visit from Scotland Yard.

Now in wild flight across war-torn Britain, Thayer fell under the swing of "the Abbott pendulum," as he called it—a cycle of mania and depression eliminating sense and self. After a brief stay in Glasgow, Thayer departed again, this time for America, leaving his colleague Sargent without a word. He'd left behind only a suitcase. Expecting to find detailed plans for the implementation of Thayer's designs, Sargent opened the suitcase at a meeting with British officials only to discover a few drawings and an old Norfolk jacket with rags pinned to it.

This jettisoned jacket had belonged to the late William James. William James Jr., Thayer's student, gave it to the artist on his father's death. James Sr. famously observed, "a man's vision is the great fact about him." It's possible to imagine Thayer wrapped in the philosopher's coat aboard a storm-gray ocean liner. In certain moments, he was known to refer to himself in the third person. One wonders if this was done in silent acknowledgment of the phantasmic forces of his delusions emitting a kind of perceptual twin that followed him across the world. Watching dawn compose the Atlantic in emergencies of white, red, and blue, the sun must've seemed a double agent bearing the dark conspiracy of the artist's soul.

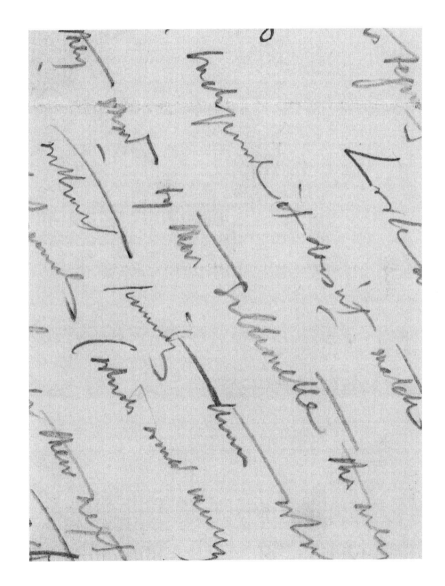

49

TRANSPARENT PROTESTS

A sunflower is a century.

    A shadow its country.

A season is a verdict.

    A valley an oath.

Who has described it—

    twilight's dream

        impoverishing the mind's?

My landscape died of winter.

    My landscape died

      where redleaves

        eat through snow.

It was an insect and a fable.

    It was a fever and a place.

It tightened its hate into a sunflower

    and became a man.

His tangled limbs

    were homily.

His path drowned

    in wildflowers.

Every day the sun crawls

    into his mouth

        and bares its teeth.

It loves the quartermoon in May.

It swallows noonlight,

    tastes the green of labor,

        the gray of industry.

The first money was leather.

    It was born and died.

It had a name,

    a home, a face.

Even money had

      a mother and father.

Its goodeye was a dream.

      Its blindeye a totem.

Every day it buried

      time's decrepit image in its own.

Every day I paint a sunflower without eyes.

            I paint its shadow;

                I leave it where I please.

            I leave it in my canvas;

                It loves dusk's falling forms.

            It loves the painter's despair—

                which is the inside of light.

            It loves the robin's death—

which is a sleep

of thorn and bramble.

When the artist sees his shadow

in the grass,

he thinks the sun

is dead.

When he finds a deadbird

in a ditch,

he digs a graveyard

with each brushstroke:

First there was the sunflower I pretended to ignore.
Then there was the sunflower I pretended to see.

The sunflower digs the ground.

It leaves the body.

It grows from cadence calls,

which lead the tongue

from silence

to its vanishing.

OCCIPITAL

see these greens

pressed tight

between the dead

leaf scarlet

drinks you in

dark of wing

eyes from the ground^{*up*}

first winter then

unanswerable yel-

low throat

the whole bare

American body

eats twilight

from its sparrowed seed

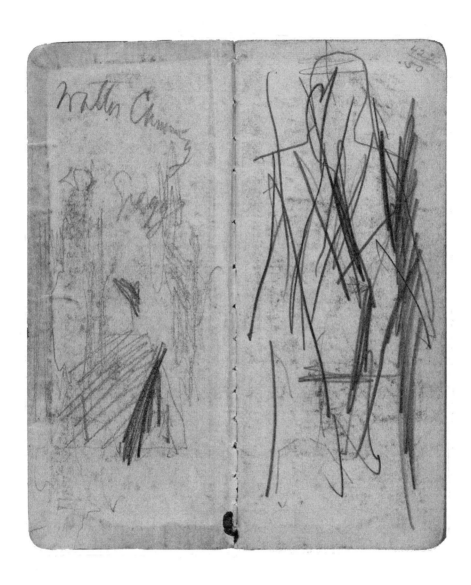

55

TRANSPARENT PROTESTS

a hard wind

                 blows in the

                           boughs;

the   sun   is

         the   flower

of   my   dreams;

                    that sun   of

                        sudden

                         inscape;

is day its deep migration?

night is

fall-

ing fast;

I push   away

from   the   sun;

I see only

the sun;

light-

filled

canvas

barb-

ed wire

in wild iris;

"I want none

       of this

           violence"

               the sun says

          and the

                people say,

       "but the sun is also a child of day"—

blackwillow

     peering

             into space—

it hides it gleams

      like a moon's

           white wake;

cracking branch

                                                                    arterial plain

of matter—

                                        the sun;

            my father was

                                                                    a sparrow

my field is bare—

                        on the bodies   of the dead

                                                                    it is opened

                                                                    like a door—

I can't get rid of

        it by looking;

I can't tell it from

        a ringing   in my ears;

                "no man has ever died in America"

                the sun says—

        when I speak I fear it;

                when I'm frightened I cannot speak;

beyond the reach of words,

                free of form and color;

                                                        if the sun were

a man I'd kill him;

                                                        if the sun were

a soldier I'd turn and shoot;

                                                        unwilling sun

                                                        deluged sun

my brother was

                                                        a tree

                                                        a blue-eyed

grass the temperature of the leaves

the blacksnake

the sun

I had lost sight

of, or never perceived;

if a tree is in

the way it's cut down;

if a man is in

the way he's the sun;

the clouds are executioners;

yes my speech

        is strange—

                the fact is

                I'm a mystic—

                        so I go along

                        like nothing's happened—

                        the wind raves;

                        the sky is filled

                        with mute thunder—

I've prowled its

                                        full existence—

my breath stars

                              the darkness;

                    a gaping figure

                                        storms my field

of vision;

                                        the sun breaks

                    like a leaf

CARNIVOROUS VERISIMILITUDES

Looking to the sight,

    I am lost.

Folded over dogday

    cicada nighthawk sun-

        fleck, an instant split

    within the lark.

    In the rhizomatic

        motion of flight,

    crown and nape

    are paradox—

        vivid dislocations

    the color of time.

    Which is doubled,

        a palimpsest,

    and twice obliterated.

        Have I begun to see?

Or perceived that nothing,

    pulverized in a moment

crossed with sea

    and fate.

        Through it, I sift and seed

          and seed and sift.

      My canvas is planted

        in its composition.

      A veiled route trapped

        in the black mirror

    of representation.

        Under the machine-

          like utterance of dusk,

           a glance throws

             it back

           against

             its origin.

Is daylight

      its philosophy

or nature?

            Does it reinscribe

            the frame?

                      Or has

                      it coalesced,

                      flower and seed,

                      around chronologies

                      of verge

                      and surface?

            Doubling back through

                life's dissolving

                greenery,

            I gather in aesthetic

                    consequence.

                Is what's rendered

            growth or sediment?

Trespass, graft, or theft.

Within the image,

a figure neither

ground nor disappearance.

When I face it,

have I turned away?

When I give it form,

I glimpse the idea

of the present as

it approaches at the

speed of vision

the fact of

its having been.

So the moment works

backward to itself.

And in a drift of

thought and weather,

it dreams through paper

moon and clouded ridge.

RED BIRD

I shall mother
(gun and ammunition)

the sun the whole

self floods:

2 beautiful finches

1 yellow warbler

[*moon*   *moon*   *moon*]

the most perfect of deaths

concave in its fraternity

NOTES

"Fugitive Depth": The phrase "for what is looking" (page 16) is borrowed from Susan Howe's *Singularities.* "Burst like a stream / making a world how large do you think it is / and how far?" (page 17) is excerpted from John Cage's *M,* from the work "Song."

"Photograph of Abbott Handerson Thayer's *Portrait of Kate Thayer,* 1888–89": The words "it seems such an indignity" and "changed face" (page 35) are from Abbott Thayer's letters to Joe Evans, 1891.

"[In November 1915, Abbott Thayer traveled from Monadnock . . .]": The quote "a man's vision is the great fact about him" (page 47) is from William James's *A Pluralistic Universe.*

*

In this writing, I am indebted to the following scholars and authors who wrote so deeply and insightfully of Abbott Thayer's life and work: Nelson C. White, Mary Fuertes Boynton, Elizabeth Lee, Roy R. Behrens, Alexander Nemerov, Richard Murray, and Sharon Kingsland.

ACKNOWLEDGMENTS

I am deeply grateful to the following individuals who helped in ways big and small in the realization of this work: Joe Lennon, Laura Wetherington, Kevin Killian, Tim Earley, Denise Newman, Matt Shears, Gloria Frym, Lucas Rivera and Sharon Zetter, Burt Ritchie, Scott Howard, Susan Howe, the wonderful Stephanie G'Schwind and her team at the Center for Literary Publishing, Natalie Lois Rogers, Mom, Dad, and Jake.

I would like also to thank the editors of the following journals for publishing earlier versions of these poems: *Volt,* the *Seattle Review, OmniVerse, New American Writing, The The Poetry, Word for/ Word, Noö Journal, Conjunctions, BlazeVOX,* and *Otoliths.*

Thanks as well to the Archives of American Art, of the Smithsonian Institution, for generously granting permission to reproduce images from the Abbott Handerson Thayer and Thayer Family papers, 1851–1999.

This book is set in Garamond
by The Center for Literary Publishing
at Colorado State University.

Copyediting by Katherine Indermaur.
Proofreading by Susannah Lodge-Rigal.
Book design and typesetting by Daniel Schonning.
Cover design by Michelle LaCrosse.
Printing by BookMobile.